**The Turtle & The Crane**

Copyright © 2024 Daniel Murray

All rights reserved.

ISBN: 978-0-6453665-2-5

Published by Empathic Consulting 2024

Bribie Island, QLD , Australia

No parts of this publication may be reproduced, stored in a retrieval system, or transmitted in any form or by any means, electronic, mechanical, photocopying, recording, or otherwise, without the prior written permission of the copyright owner.

This book is sold subject to the condition that it shall not, by way of trade or otherwise be resold, hired out, or otherwise circulated without the publisher's prior consent in any form of binding or cover other than that in which it is published and without a similar condition including this condition being imposed on the subsequent purchaser. Under no circumstances may any part of this book be photocopied for resale.

This is a work of fiction. Any similarity between the characters and situations within its pages is unintentional and co-incidental.

**Illustrations by** Bárbarabá

Dedicated to the memory of Beryl Murray, my Nana and the kindest person I've ever known…

# The Turtle & The Crane

# By Daniel Murray

In a land filled with green forests and tall mountains, there were three sparkling lakes. In these lakes lived a Turtle and a Crane.

The Turtle loved swimming in the clear waters, diving amongst the fish and munching on yummy seaweed.

The Crane, with his long legs and sharp beak, was great at catching fish. He liked to dance along the shores, peering through the weeds and hunting for his next meal.

One day, dark clouds covered the sky, and it started to rain. It rained and rained for 30 days non-stop! The lakes grew bigger and deeper until they joined together into one huge, deep sea.

The Turtle was excited about this new, big sea. She had so many new places to explore, new friends to meet, and tasty grasses to snack on. But for the Crane, this was a big problem.

The shallows had vanished and the water was too deep for him to stand and catch fish. He was getting very hungry and tired, circling in the sky with nowhere to land.

The Turtle looked up and saw the Crane flying above. He looked lost, tired and hungry. The Turtle stopped exploring and swam to the surface.

"Hey Mr. Crane, come stand on my shell." she called out. The Crane looked down in surprise. He gently landed on the Turtle's big, strong shell and rested. He then looked into the water and was able to catch a few fish to eat. He slowly became stronger again.

Every day, the Turtle would swim to the surface, and the Crane would stand on her shell to catch fish.

The Turtle didn't explore as much as she used to, but helping the Crane made her feel good. They became friends, sharing stories and spending time swimming across the top of the water.

Many years passed, and then the weather changed again. This time, the sun shone so brightly for many, many days. There were no clouds in the sky, and it didn't rain for a very long time. The hot days made the lakes dry up and shrink. The three great lakes became just a lot of small, muddy puddles.

Now, the Crane was having a great time. He could walk in the shallow water and easily catch the trapped fish. But the Turtle was in trouble. She found it hard to move in the sticky mud and couldn't find enough food. She was very hungry and tired.

The Crane saw his old friend struggling and remembered how the Turtle had helped him after the floods. Now it was his turn to help. He swooped in and gently picked up the Turtle in his claws. The Turtle looked up to see her old friend smiling as he pulled her out of the thick mud.

They flew together over the puddles, looking for patches of seaweed. He took her to many puddles each day so she could find food in the muddy waters.

After the drought, the lakes filled up again. The Turtle and the Crane had become the best of friends. They shared many adventures and always helped each other out when they needed.

All the animals around the lakes talked about the Turtle and the Crane. They were amazed the two very different creatures could be such good friends and help each other

The Turtle and the Crane taught everyone that if you can help others when they need it, you should.

It is always important to be kind to those different from you. You never know when you might need them to help you.

And that's the story of the Turtle and the Crane.

# The Turtle & The Crane

The story of the Turtle & the Crane was inspired by a statue I came across while traveling in Vietnam. It inspired me for many years in looking for ways to support others. It also helped me park my ego, and accept help when I needed it. We all must make an effort to look beyond our own interests and help others, especially those who are different from us.

If we can help others,
we should.

## About the Author

Daniel Murray is a sought-after motivational Keynote Speaker and Business Consultant currently located in Bribie Island, Australia.

Through his experience working with some of the biggest companies in Australia and New Zealand, he has seen firsthand that building empathy and connection is vital for the future of business. With a background in mathematics and strategy, and a passion for understanding people, he is able to blend diverse concepts to create ground breaking ideas.

Daniel speaks at businesses, schools and conferences and also conducts experiential workshops to teach people how to develop Empathic Leadership, build an understanding of the rational and emotional needs of others and then provide guidance and support to foster a flexible, resourceful and high-performing workplace.

empathicconsulting.com

www.ingramcontent.com/pod-product-compliance
Lightning Source LLC
Chambersburg PA
CBHW051216290426
44109CB00021B/2473